The Journey

Unexpected yet Necessary

Antoria Jones

Copyright © 2023 Antoria Jones

Lisa Nicole Publishing
Lisanicolealexander.com
Gotha, FL 34734

Printed in the United States of America

ISBN: 979-8-9878940-1-9

Introduction

For many years, as a Christian, John 10:27 - My sheep hear my voice, and I know them, and they follow me, was not completely applied to my life. I did a lot of listening. Unfortunately, I cannot say my ears were attentive to the Lord. Fear was the amplifier that led me. I lived life afraid of God, people, and the enemy. Because of this, I held a lot within the borders of my fears. I did not want to be judged by God, abandoned by people, or attacked by the enemy. I was even afraid of myself. Weird, I know. But can you relate?

These fears caused me to go into hiding. I lived a life of fear and anxiety. I was far from perfect, but I never disclosed those weaknesses until there was no more hiding. When my life turned upside down, it caused me to be exposed. How you may ask? By confession. My first step was to be real with myself, God, loved ones, and now with you.

This journal is a journey filled with my testimonies, and I invited you to journal alongside me. Here is an opportunity for us to be real together. All our days are not sunshine and roses. It takes strength to admit that. As you read the pages of my heart, I pray you will have the boldness to express your truth. It is time to be an open book.

The Bible says in Revelation 12:11, we overcome him by the blood of the Lamb and by the WORD OF OUR TESTIMONY, and they loved not their lives unto the death.

Day of Living Beyond Fears

This poem is the essence of why this devotional was written. As a Christian, I did everything to try to make things seem perfect in my life. I was the rule follower, faithful friend, encourager, forgiver, and giver, all SOUNDS great, but there is nothing impressive about a "mask." I lived afraid. I did not want to be left alone, so I became what everyone needed. Fear caused me to stay within the boards. It trapped me. I operated under its thumbprint for too long. Fear was the very thing that caused me to live life as a perfectionist.

My life was a mess, but I painted what I wanted everyone to see. I did not want the cracks within my walls to be seen. Through one of the most significant events in my life, I grew to understand God knows we are real people making real mistakes and that we need a real God.

Between these covers are pages of me as a daughter, choosing to come out of darkness (deal with life and choices) and doing life with my father. Trust me, life, at times, can seem unfair. It can present us with blows we felt unprepared for, left to deal with the rubbish of the aftermath. These pages are filled with highs and lows, but I only see victories with God. I pray, as you read, you will find trust for today and hope for tomorrow.

I pray you are reminded of the faithfulness of God in your life. According to Romans 8:28, He makes ALL things work together for our good. Do you believe it?

In what ways can you live beyond your fears?

_____

_____

_____

_____

_____

_____

_____

_____

_____

_____

_____

_____

_____

_____

_____

_____

_____

_____

_____

_____

New Day of Peace

Exodus 14:13

For many years, I would get so entangled with the cares of this world. It would consume me. I lived with false burdens, anxiety, and fears. I did not know how it felt to be at peace. To be honest, peace was not a part of my vocabulary. Don't get me wrong, I enjoyed happy moments, but they were all void of PEACE! I walked afraid. My eyes were always looking over my shoulders, wondering, what's next?

None of us can say we have MASTERED anything, but Jesus has. To God alone, be all the glory. Everything may not be perfect, but He is. Due to this truth, we can breathe and wait.

Friend, be confident in his ability to see you through life challenges. You are called to stand just as the children of Israel were in Exodus 14:13. It says Moses answered the people, "Do not be afraid (be at peace). Stand firm(believe), and you will see the deliverance (rescue) the LORD will bring you today. The Egyptians (anything against God's plans) you see today, you will never see again.

Let this be your hope and truth. Let it be where you find peace. Yes, it's your new reality.

In what areas of your life do you need to ask God to give you Peace?

_____

_____

_____

_____

_____

_____

_____

_____

_____

_____

_____

_____

_____

_____

_____

_____

_____

New Day of Waiting

Waiting is a hard task to accept at times. I'm reminded of the children of Israel when Moses went up the mountain, and they were waiting for an answer from God. They started out strong. It was like starting a race they were all in until the timeframe did not meet their expectations.

Instead of waiting, they decided to create their own way. They started committing sins WHILE being children of God. I believe this happened because they simply lost hope. They started complaining, became distracted, and allowed their flesh to take over. When a person loses hope, they have the potential to become idle.

There is danger in idleness. It's a battle I've fought and have not always been successful in. The Bible says, in Proverbs 16:27, idle hands are the devil's workshop (sin is readily available); idle lips are his mouthpiece (spoken words contrary to the word of God). I understand the ability to sin during times like these. I ask God's grace and mercy to be with us as He promised. For those that have fallen, I pray against condemnation. I pray for spiritual recovery. Lastly, I am praying for us to keep busy with the work of the Father. Wait well for an answer in faith. It's coming.

How can you honor God in your waiting?

_____

_____

_____

_____

_____

_____

_____

_____

_____

_____

_____

_____

_____

_____

_____

_____

New Day of the Mix Up

One of my daughter's favorite movies is High School Musical. One scene from this movie went a little something like this. Troy wanted to sing, yet he was a basketball star. It was not the norm for a basketball player to sing, especially in a musical! It was against the rules or norms of high school. Well, the knowledge about this got out. It turned the school upside down. Due to Troy's reveal, others broke the status quo, too.

This scene mirrors, in some ways, the lady at the well. She knew all about sticking to traditions, rules, and or stigmas carried on her shoulders. Then she met Jesus. He was not naive about the practices. He was fully aware of what the woman carried. He did not allow anything to hinder meeting with her. It was his day to mix it up! Here she was not only carrying others' baggage but her own, as well. So here we have a Samaritan, and He a Jew. She was known for being with multiple men, yet she was meeting the Son of God.

She was spiritually thirsty, and he was the Living Water. If that's not mixing things up, I don't know what is! He mixed it up so well that other Samaritans joined in, just as with High School Musical. It's funny how watching a Disney movie can bring out some expected norms. Freedom is contagious and has nothing to do with normalcy. Allow him to mix some things up this week in your life and bring others along for the ride!

How has God been "mixing" things up in your life?

_____

_____

_____

_____

_____

_____

_____

_____

_____

_____

_____

_____

_____

_____

_____

_____

_____

_____

_____

_____

_____

_____

New Day of the Removal

I have second-guessed God's love for me due to things I've experienced. I've blamed Him because I did not understand Him. This lack of understanding led me to picture all the hurts, disappointments, and shame I experienced as tattoos plastered on the Master's face. It stopped me in my tracks.

I asked myself, "would you freely tattoo all the wrong things done against you (both by others and yourself) on your face?" I would not. I would not want to see myself that way. This is the same with the Father. He wants us to see him accurately. We will never accomplish this if we envision him misconstrued. You may be like me if you are still reading this devotional. We both desire to see God as the loving Father. The only way this will happen is through the eyes of LOVE, which is through his son Jesus Christ!

Lord, forgive us for projecting on you all of our disappointments. You are far too good, and you are good to us. Help us to comprehend with all the saints the width, length, depth, and height of your love towards us Eph 3:18.

In what ways have you misconstrued who God really is?
How can you ask Him to show you who He really is?

_____

_____

_____

_____

_____

_____

_____

_____

_____

_____

_____

_____

_____

_____

_____

_____

New Day of Living by Truth

There are dangers associated with living out of our experiences, good or bad. Don't allow your decisions for today to be dictated by your successes or failures of yesterday. Our experiences in life do not make it TRUTH. It's just that; our experiences. Life experiences could be moments of victories and failures. Living there can cause some things to happen.

Focusing on victories can build self-reliance, have former days syndrome, or make us boastful. Those that focus on past failures have fears of tomorrow, and their feet may become crippled hindering movement, develop a lack of trust, or live as a victim. Both extremes are dangerous! It's funny, though, because we tend to give advice when we are like this and produce others just like us...scary.

No matter what we've encountered, there is only ONE truth, and that's the Word of God. Let's allow it to be our standard. Our experiences or circumstances can change, but His word remains the same. Grace is intended for the present. We need grace for today, not for yesterday; it's gone. That manna is dried up. God has a fresh loaf for today. Paul was a man that allowed this to be true for himself. Look at Hebrews 12. It's time to lay it ALL down to receive all he has for us.

What TRUTH does the Word of God say about you?

_____

_____

_____

_____

_____

_____

_____

_____

_____

_____

_____

_____

_____

_____

_____

_____

_____

_____

_____

New Day of Change

A Time and Season for everything

I was a person that wanted everything to remain the same. Even if pain was an outcome of things not changing, it was okay. Change was a scary place for me. I held on tight. With all honesty, change is still not something I look forward to. I found myself fighting for the very things I knew I needed to let go of. I would do everything in my power to keep things together or in order.

When things changed, I felt powerless. I would walk with the bricks of this burden on my shoulders. The bricks of trying to keep things the same and avoiding change at all costs. It is a heavy price to pay. I had to decide to enjoy the journey and embrace the changes. They would come anyway. Change is inevitable!!!! There is a time and a season for everything under the heavens- Ecclesiastes 3:1. Yet, all change may not feel good, But God makes all changes for our good; change will come.

Father God, give us the grace to embrace change. There is a time and a season for everything under the sun. Change may be inevitable, but we remain stable in You.

In what ways can you better embrace change?

_____

_____

_____

_____

_____

_____

_____

_____

_____

_____

_____

_____

_____

_____

_____

_____

Day of Character

I'm just thinking about all the things we can put on, like perfume, lotion, clothes, hair accessories, shoes, glasses, jewelry, etc., which are all good and, at times, greatly appreciated. Yet, your character is one of the greatest things you will ever put on.

Many would say they don't care what others think of them, but we were not called to live in a bubble. We were created to do life with people. Our character is a major determinant of how successful we will be in this area. Character can be so stylish that others would wear it (imitate), or it can be torn, stained, and undesirable (repellent) to someone.

We can put more emphasis on that which fades away. It's time to refocus. Our names are attached to our characters. I desire for my name to remain on the earth after I'm long gone. I want to be known as a follower of Christ, a carrier of the fruits of the spirit, a soul winner, a Bible-believing, dedicated mother, a lover of people, a loyal friend, honest, relentless, overcomer, passionate, compassionate, forgiving and the list goes on.

Jesus, Mary, Ruth, Peter, Paul, and many others in the Bible are spoken of daily. What will your character speak concerning you once you can't speak for yourself?

What do you want your character to speak concerning you?

_____

_____

_____

_____

_____

_____

_____

_____

_____

_____

_____

_____

_____

_____

_____

_____

_____

_____

_____

_____

_____

_____

Day of Patience

Wait for God's promise instead of going your own way. In Acts 1:4, the Bible says, "and while being in their company and eating with them, he (Jesus) commanded them NOT to leave Jerusalem but to WAIT for what the Father had promised, of which you have heard me speak."

Wait? Yes, wait! Waiting on God is not a passive position to take. It requires patience, strength, and endurance. You tell me when those words ever came easy! Our way will always lead to destruction, heartache, and or pain. We serve ourselves best by following God's plan and remaining in time with him.

I'm determined to walk with God in every season of my life. I don't want to run ahead or drag behind. Each step that He takes, I want to be by His side.

What does walking in season with God mean? What does it look like? It is denying self! It is allowing His will to be established in our lives. It's us learning to move to the rhythm of his drum.

God's goodness is promised to those who wait patiently for him! No matter how long, it's worth it. Regardless of how hopeless things may appear. No matter what others may say. Even when it seems to cost you everything, don't stop believing! "God can do far more abundantly than all that we ask or think, according to his power at work within us" (Ephesians 3:20). When we wait for him, we will never be disappointed. Trust Him! His ways are perfect!

In what ways can you be more patient while waiting on God?

_____

_____

_____

_____

_____

_____

_____

_____

_____

_____

_____

_____

_____

_____

_____

_____

_____

_____

_____

_____

Day of Community

This is my life. I love people! This was not always my testimony due to being wronged throughout my life. I was the one that had my guard up. It seemed, at the time, I was protecting myself, but in reality, it was a prison. It kept me from experiencing life to the fullest. We were never meant to do life alone. It is wisdom to evaluate who you are walking with, of course! Your crew can promote life or create a road of death. I am talking about a me against the world mentality. It was not until I let God into my heart that I realized some things. I may get hurt, things may not go my way, and dealing with people can be a little sketchy, but it beats walking alone any day. Community works!

How can you increase your supportive community?

_____

_____

_____

_____

_____

_____

_____

_____

_____

_____

_____

_____

_____

_____

_____

_____

_____

_____

_____

Day of Distancing is Over

Will we appreciate those that serve in all the places we currently can't go? Will we embrace those we neglected before? Will we appreciate the server that had an attitude that we thought didn't deserve a tip?

Will we appreciate the homeless sitting on a bench?

What about that flight attendant that told us what to do?

Will we appreciate workers that create opportunities for memories with our families, but their lines are too long?

Will we stop forgetting those we say "we just don't get along with"?

Will we, instead of calling, pull up and meet?

Or will we keep our distance because it's who we really want to be?

Community is where my heart is.

I appreciate you; can you appreciate me?

We were never meant to be alone.

It's not about who's right and who's wrong.

Let's forgive and move on.

It's not about my family only.

Do life together. Don't live behind a closed door.

Love God. Love people.

Walk together and keep the peace.

Appreciate those that make life happen for you

Leave no one behind.

No voluntary social distancing is allowed.

Appreciation and compassion for others are on the frontlines

How can you increase your community?

_____

_____

_____

_____

_____

_____

_____

_____

_____

_____

_____

_____

_____

_____

_____

_____

_____

_____

Day of Letting Go

Testimony time

For many years, I would get entangled with all of its cares. It would consume me. I lived with false burdens, anxiety, and fear. I did not know how it felt to be at peace. To be honest, peace was not a part of my vocabulary. Don't get me wrong, I enjoyed happy moments, but they were all void of PEACE! I walked afraid. My eyes were always looking over my shoulders, wondering, "what's next?"

I can't tell you I've MASTERED anything, but I am not where I used to be. It was not until I found hope in Jesus, the Unshakeable One, that I began to have moments like these. Everything may not be perfect, but He is. Due to this truth, I can breathe and wait. I am confident in his ability to see me through life's challenges. I've found that sometimes I am called to stand just as the children of Israel were called to in Exodus 14:13. It says Moses answered the people, "Do not be afraid(be at peace). Stand firm(believe), and you will see the deliverance(rescue) the LORD will bring you today. The Egyptians(corona) you see today you will never see again.

If you need peace, please know I am praying for you as I pray for myself. We are all walking this journey.

What are some things you need to let go of?

Day of Waiting Again

The words below were written as we faced coronavirus but are for anyone that finds themselves waiting.

Waiting is a hard task to accept at times. I'm reminded of the Children of Israel when Moses went up the mountain, and they were waiting for an answer. They started out strong. It was like starting a race they were all in until the timeframe did not meet their expectations.

Instead of waiting, they decided to create their own way. They started committing sins WHILE being Children of God. I believe this happened because they simply lost hope. They started complaining, becoming distracted, allowing their flesh to take over, etc. When a person loses hope, they have the potential to become idle.

There is danger in idleness. Truth, it's a battle I've fought and have not always been successful in. The Bible says, in Proverbs 16:27, idle hands are the devil's workshop (sin is readily available); idle lips are his mouthpiece (spoken words contrary to the Word of God). I understand the ability to sin during times like these. I ask God's grace and mercy to be with us as He promised. For those that have fallen, I pray against condemnation. I pray for spiritual recovery. Lastly, I am praying for us to keep busy. That we wait well for an answer in faith, it's coming.

In what ways can you choose to wait "well"?

_____

_____

_____

_____

_____

_____

_____

_____

_____

_____

_____

_____

_____

_____

_____

_____

_____

_____

_____

_____

Day of Uncomfortableness

My comforts held me back for years. I was unaware that being comfortable was really fear dressed up in disguise for me. Once the truth was exposed, I wanted to hold on to my comforts. Why? Because we had become friends! I was used to them being around. Well, I've decided to get comfortable with being uncomfortable. This is the only way to LIVE OUT LOUD ON PURPOSE! I have things in my heart that will never happen as long as I hold tight to my fears or, should I say, comforts!

I am a person who really does not enjoy change, but as an adult, I recognize it is necessary. I guess I experienced so much change as a child that I related it to being unstable or a failure altogether. As I grew, I would make a plan and hold fast to it like a security blanket. Sometimes, I would get so stuck trying to achieve, maintain and just live that I could not enjoy the journey! I would do everything humanly possible to see the plan or vision come to fruition in my life. Of course, this required little to no reliance on God. Even now, as a Christian, I remind myself that the vision is still the same; I'm just taking another route at times. I plan my days, but now I'm WILLING to say "away with my details" if needed. This scripture says it best. Many are the plans of man, but the purposes of God shall prevail- Proverbs 19:21. This knowing is the confidence I need. I've found He's better at details than I am.

How have your comforts held you back?

_____

_____

_____

_____

_____

_____

_____

_____

_____

_____

_____

_____

_____

_____

_____

_____

_____

_____

_____

_____

Day of Singleness

May I encourage anyone single out there...?

Something I'm learning about guarding the heart. The heart does not always get it right. It relies on us to confirm that which is truth. Once we confirm, the gates of the heart open.

With that being said, we are limited in our knowledge. As singles, we have an opportunity to rely on the One that SEES and KNOWS all. Giving the Father the authority to confirm or disapprove of any potential relationship in our lives doesn't make us vulnerable but valuable.

The Bible says in 1 Samuel 16:7, But the Lord said to Samuel, "Do not look on his appearance or the height of his stature, because I have rejected him. For the Lord sees not as man sees: man looks on the outward appearance, but the Lord looks on the heart."

I put this verse here to show how God looks at the heart of man. Samuel was about to anoint the wrong man for a position that he was not called to. How many of you have given someone a title that did not belong to that person? God understands we can get caught up on outer appearances (6'0ft, bearded, suit, oh my!), but that's not what makes a man acceptable in God's sight.

Kingdom relationships are to bring glory to His name. He even based His relationship with the Church as an example of how marriage should be. What has he called you to? Is the person suitable for the call? That question goes both ways. Take time to evaluate and ask the Lord. Trust the Father's plans for your life. He knows. Trust him!!!

Note: Just because God rejects a person as your spouse does not mean he rejected them altogether. It's plain and simple the person is not for you. No hard feelings. Rejoice and keep it moving.

How can you glorify God in your season of singleness?

_____

_____

_____

_____

_____

_____

_____

_____

_____

_____

_____

Day of Joy

There have been times I've felt weak. Moments when I wanted to give up. I did not know my soul required joy. I needed joy at that very moment. Joy is tied to thanksgiving. When I decided to thank God, something happened! Joy entered the room. I would find strength for another day's journey.

Having joy is an option, but the wrong decision not to accept it can be catastrophic. Having joy is CRUCIAL. According to Nehemiah 8:10, the Bible says, "the joy of the Lord is our strength."

Typically, as people, we want to be happy. But happiness comes and goes, but joy remains.

Joy is everlasting!

It is not of this world!

Joy comes from God alone.

Jot down moments of JOY!

Day of Moving Forward

So much can change from one year to the next. Life is either moving as expected, or there is a completely new rendition. Life has a way of presenting the new. Here's the good news. The Lord has given all we need that pertains to life and godliness, according to 2 Peter 1:3. He empowers us by His Spirit to MOVE FORWARD, ask Paul (Philippians 3:4). He makes every mountain low in our lives. Although it's time for something new, we can sometimes find our heads hanging low. May I encourage you with Psalms 3:3 as you navigate the new? God is the lifter of your head. May the Lord, by his grace, lift your head as you boldly move forward. Live again, believe again, trust again, and get moving again!

What things do you need to let go of so you can move forward?

_____

_____

_____

_____

_____

_____

_____

_____

_____

_____

_____

_____

_____

_____

_____

_____

_____

_____

_____

Day of Continuing On

Giving up is not an option for me. I really want to see what the end will be. I will hold fast to the confession of my faith (in every area of life), for it holds great reward- Hebrews 10:23!

Although I may have to wait for it, I will wait. I have too much riding on my "YES"! Here is something I keep before me. The road is not always easy, but it is worth it. Fight the good fight of faith!

What YES have you given to God that you are waiting on Him to fulfill?

_____

_____

_____

_____

_____

_____

_____

_____

_____

_____

_____

_____

_____

_____

_____

_____

_____

_____

_____

_____

Day of Forgiveness

Forgiveness is a key that unlocks closed doors. It's time to check the keys on your keychain. It just may fit!

"And when you stand praying (making your request), if you HOLD ANYTHING against anyone, FORGIVE them, so that your Father in heaven may forgive you your sins." Mark 11:25

It's time to obtain what's behind the closed doors.

Who do you need to forgive?

_____

_____

_____

_____

_____

_____

_____

_____

_____

_____

_____

_____

_____

_____

_____

_____

_____

_____

_____

Day of Waiting Again

Waiting is something I naturally don't like to do. I'm a person that makes it happen. This attitude puts undesired pressure on me, but I still find myself operating in this way. Of course, it does not remain in the physical this attitude transfers right into spiritual things. Over the years, I've learned more than ever I am not in control, and truthfully, I really don't want to be. I am at peace when I sit and just listen. My prayer is, Lord help me to grow in waiting on you.

In John 4, The woman at the well had a water pot (her truth) in hopes of receiving water. She left the well receiving so much more. The pot was her truth. She was in need. She tried to fill herself. She was doing things the only way she knew how. It's funny; once her pot was filled with water, it was never enough. She would find herself at the well repeatedly.

What may seem to us like it will take forever took a moment. When she received the truth, she was fulfilled. The Bible says it's the truth that sets us free. Upon receiving it, she was instantly healed from yesterday (life). Within the community, they saw her with the water pot. They knew why she went to the well, but she came to them with nothing in her hands. She left behind her pot; the very thing once weighed her down. She took TRUTH from her moment with Jesus, and it became her story to tell.

Write out your prayer: Lord help me to grow in my waiting on you.

_____

_____

_____

_____

_____

_____

_____

_____

_____

_____

_____

_____

_____

_____

_____

_____

_____

_____

_____

_____

Day of Life Beyond Yesterday

There are dangers associated with living out of our experiences, good or bad. Don't allow your decisions for today to be dictated by your successes or failures of yesterday. Our experiences in life do not make it TRUTH. It's just that; our experiences. Those could be moments of victories or failures. Living here can cause some things to happen.

Focusing on victories, one can become self-reliant, have former days syndrome, and be boastful. Those that focus on past failures can have fears for tomorrow and become crippled. This can hinder movement and create a lack of trust. Both are dangerous!!! It's funny, though, because we tend to give advice from this place and produce others just like us...scary. There is no judgment here. This is for me, too!

No matter what we've encountered, there is only ONE truth, and that's the Word of God. Our experiences or circumstances can change, but His word remains the same.

Grace is intended for the present. We need grace for today, not for yesterday; it's gone. That manna is dried up. God has a fresh loaf for today. Paul was a man that allowed this to be true for himself. Take a look at Hebrews 12. It's time to lay it ALL down to receive all He has for us.

What do you need to lay down to receive all Christ has for you?

_____

_____

_____

_____

_____

_____

_____

_____

_____

_____

_____

_____

_____

_____

_____

_____

_____

_____

_____

Day of One More Time

Cast your net one more time. Don't give up. Try the right side

John 21:1-6

Afterward, Jesus appeared again to his disciples by the Sea of Galilee. It happened this way: Simon Peter, Thomas (also known as Didymus), Nathanael from Cana in Galilee, the sons of Zebedee, and two other disciples were together. "I'm going out to fish," Simon Peter told them, and they said, "We'll go with you." So they went out and got into the boat, but that night they caught nothing.

Early in the morning, Jesus stood on the shore, but the disciples did not realize it was Jesus. He called out to them, "Friends, haven't you any fish?" No," they answered. He said, "Throw your net on the right side of the boat, and you will find some." When they did, they could not haul the net in because of the large number of fish.

Faith is an entity that coexists with us from birth. Faith is alive! It has movement and form. Faith is subject to change based on what we decide to believe. Anytime faith was redefined in someone's life things began to happen throughout the Bible- (the blind man received sight, the woman with an issue of blood was healed and the list goes on). Let yourself off the hook today. Redefine faith for your current season and watch God move.

How can you redefine faith for your current season?

Day of Confidence

Paul says in Philippians 4:11 he LEARNED to be content in whatever situation. 1 Timothy 6 (Amp) says that contentment comes from inner confidence in God's sufficiency. So, Paul had CONFIDENCE in God that he would not fail.

If we were to ask Paul's heart directly, I wonder how it would respond. Would it have the same response? I don't think so. I believe his heart would respond based on the events and circumstances of Paul's life.

Most of Paul's letters to the church were written from behind prison doors. The heart would not see that as God is sufficient. The heart would respond something like this: Here you are again, the Lord has left you abandoned. Paul (Antoria), you can't preach the gospel because you don't want to be attacked! I told you the last time not to trust those people. You will never be married, and you can forget about having kids. Are you watching your timeline?

This is why the Bible tells us in Jeremiah 17:9 not to follow our hearts or feelings because the heart is deceitful. It will lead you to believe what's not TRUTH. It will cause unnecessary anxiety and fear.

We know from reading about Paul what God did in and through his life. Lives were changed, he wrote a good portion of the New Testament, which impacts us today, etc. During his time, though, he had to choose to BELIEVE no matter what.

Let's feed our hearts the truth. There is more to the story.

What truths do you need to speak into your life today?

Day of Reevaluation

It's time to reevaluate the individuals in our lives. People come in two forms. There is Peter and Judas. We can see this in the Bible. Both walked, ate, and talked with Jesus. They did life with him. This is why we must pray to know who is who.

ALL hurt or pain does not equate to an individual being a Judas in our lives; ask Jesus.

Sometimes the hurt comes from unattended wounds, fears, etc. A true friend exposes bandages to promote healing. If the hurt came from a bandaid being removed, let me tell you, "it's not Judas." Value that relationship!

It may hurt, but is there a surgical procedure that does not?

Proverbs 27:6 says, wounds from a friend can be trusted, but an enemy multiplies kisses.

Take some time to reevaluate the people in your life.

Day of House Check

Do you have something in your house that if it's removed, you would know? It's that one thing that means everything to you. Maybe it's a generational item passed down from a loved one. Is it your college jacket with all your patches? Oh, I know, it's your favorite coffee cup. You know, the one no one can use? It holds just enough coffee to start your day. It keeps your coffee hot for hours. It's indeed *your* cup. It even has a name. Okay, you get the point. In life, we all have things we value, and if they went missing, we would be on the hunt for them.

In my household, that would be my children. As a mom, I can't have my eyes on them all the time. Because of this, I teach my children the importance of being accountable for each other. Sometimes, one of them will tell on the other because I did not see something happen. Truthfully, it keeps them safe and helps keep each other from trouble. This is something I pray remains with them.

Being an only child was much different. Do you know how much I got into right under my mother's nose while in the house? I was curious, so I tried things at times that I knew were wrong. Having a sibling could have prevented so much tenderness of the behind. I thought of this as I was reading. It's not enough to be named or called. We must be accounted for even while being in the house of God.

This is a reason why comparison is so dangerous. It can allow us to see a sister go astray and, due to our insecurities, say nothing. In Genesis 4:1-13, Cain was so angry and jealous of his brother Abel that he killed him. Afterward, when God asked, "Where is Abel?" Cain said he didn't know. That's when Cain asked, "Am I my brother's keeper?" But he was really saying, "My brother is not my problem." This can't be true. If there's a problem, we've been given an answer. Ladies, let's shake off comparison. We need one another! We are ALL in the same house; we are ALL called Children of God; we are ALL chosen, so let's ALL be accounted for.

This is something I tell my kids daily, "watch out for one another". Yes, we are our sisters' keeper. Are you the eyes in the house when no one else is watching?

See what an incredible quality of love the Father has shown to us, that we would [be permitted to] be named, called, and counted as the children of God! And so we are! For this reason, the world does not know us, because it did not know Him.
1 John 3:1 AMP

How can you be your sister's keeper?

_____

_____

_____

_____

_____

_____

_____

_____

_____

_____

_____

_____

_____

_____

_____

_____

Day of Living

My childhood had a lot of moving pieces. I faced things that a child should not be burdened with. I faced mental abuse from hurting adults, homelessness, starvation, a parent not showing interest, while the other parent fought for her life due to sickness. As I grew, I was so afraid of becoming some of the things I experienced that it put me on the road to becoming them. Everything was different physically, but my mindset was definitely there.

There, I lived, afraid of what tomorrow held. Afraid of failure, success, progress, stagnation, ups, downs, acceptance, rejection, love, and abandonment. The possibility of either outcome (unstable) caused my heart to fear. I had no clue what true success or relationships looked like, and who was I to accomplish such a thing? So, I walked with walls up. I would only go as far as someone else's leading or pushing.

It's funny because after giving my life to the Lord, one would think my mindset would have completely changed. Don't get me wrong; I'm not where I used to be. I've seen God's hand working in and through me, but I can't say I was living totally convinced.

I've allowed myself to walk in the same fears even as a Christian. It is our responsibility to renew our minds. Romans 12:2 tells us so.

This is done intellectually. It's like taking a prescription from a physician. I would find myself reading the word but meditating on all the wrong things.

Listen, here's a sidebar- a wrong mindset can even bring the wrong relationships into your life. Not allowing myself to operate in the fullness of who I've been called to be, allowed others with their own visions to lead me.

There is so much more life to live. I am thankful God knows how to redeem the time. I choose to set my mind on things above. I choose to believe only that which is good. I will no longer think as a double-minded person. I desire good for my life. The Father says it's all He has for me. I am living in my own book written by one hand. It's the hand that counts for me. This is me, living without rival.

In what ways do you need to renew your mind?

_____

_____

_____

_____

_____

_____

_____

_____

_____

_____

_____

_____

_____

_____

_____

_____

_____

_____

_____

Day of No Comparison

Comparison is not the source of inspiration!!!

What is inspiration? It is the process of being mentally stimulated to do or feel something, especially to do something creative.

For years, I questioned God why I was here. I had no clue as to why I had been created. Did God forget about me? Comparisons could have been the culprit to my not knowing. During those times, I found myself comparing myself to others around me. I was never good enough, beautiful enough, articulate enough, or smart enough. I simply was not enough. The funny but not so funny thing was I surrounded myself with others, that fed that part of how I was.

How could I dream or have inspiration if I believed that I was not enough? If we want to be inspired or walk in the calling God has for us individually, we must let go of comparison. We are not the same. Even if we are both called to be chefs, it does not mean we will have the same items on our menus. Even if we have the same items, it does not mean we will use the same ingredients. Walk in your differences because we need *you*!

Your individuality is an answer to someone's problem. Be the FULL you! Be the ANSWER!

How can you begin today to walk in your individuality?

_____

_____

_____

_____

_____

_____

_____

_____

_____

_____

_____

_____

_____

_____

_____

_____

_____

_____

Day of the Print

Although we share some similarities, such as being a woman, we don't have the same fingerprints. We were created to SHINE! Our display of uniqueness shows God's GREATNESS! It shows his ability to do something great with no need to duplicate. He's not like man. We will take someone's idea, change one thing about it, and call it original. God's not like that. Walking in the truth of who God has created you to be is not pride. It's not bringing glory to ourselves but to God. It's Him that gifted us in such a way. Now, ladies, it's time to display your thumbprint so the world may see.

Let your light shine before others, that they may see your good deeds and glorify your Father in heaven.
Matthew 5:16

In what ways has God made you unique?

Day of Actions

Patience has nothing to do with TIME. It has everything to do with our ACTIONS while we are waiting. The time is just that, "a period of time."

How we act while we wait shows the true position of our hearts. Are we fearful? Are we tempted to manipulate to obtain our desired outcome? Are we complaining? Are we comparing ourselves to others? Are we full of peace? Are we assured God is working on our behalf? Are we faithful to the process? Are we celebrating the wins of others? The list can go on.

See, our actions express our patience, not time. Lord, help us demonstrate true patience. Lord, HELP ME!

But the fruit of the Spirit [the result of His presence within us] is love [unselfish concern for others], joy, [inner] peace, patience [not the ability to wait, but how we act while waiting], kindness, goodness, faithfulness, gentleness, self-control. Against such things, there is no law.

Galatians 5:23 AMP

Which He will bring about in His own time—He who is the blessed and only Sovereign [the absolute Ruler], the King of those who reign as kings and Lord of those who rule as Lords, He alone possesses immortality [absolute exemption from death] and lives in unapproachable light, whom no man has ever seen or can see. To Him be honor and eternal power and dominion! Amen.

1 Timothy 6:15-16 AMP

I thought as I read this scripture over and over this morning. These words stood out, God is the King of kings, and He is the Lord of Lords. It's the word THE...

An officer of the law is known as a law enforcer, but that does not mean they were THE officer that responded to the call at 6:17 this morning. Although a doctor delivers babies, it does not mean that they delivered mine. My question is, where is THE one? See, sometimes titles can have us all mixed up, too.

Just because someone holds a title does not mean they are THE one. This is why God is without rival. He understands there are those that operate under names, but he is THE name, THE King, THE Lord, etc.
See, when we know who He is, we will not get bent out of shape when someone else holds the title, too. There is and only will be ONE you. I am THE only Antoria Germese. I truly can say that and not be conceited. We must live without rival and just BE!

We must stand no matter who else could possibly hold the same title. God teaches us to do just that. He's called us to be confident in ourselves through him.

In what ways can you ask God to increase your confidence?

_____

_____

_____

_____

_____

_____

_____

_____

_____

_____

_____

_____

_____

_____

_____

_____

_____

_____

Day of Standby

As a youth, altercations seemed to find my cousin all the time. Because of this, as cousins, we would always be together. We never let each other out of sight. As adults, we've talked about those times, and my cousin shared, "she never concerned herself about LOSING." She understood her abilities, and she also had cousins standing by.

I am not sharing this story to promote living a life of altercation. I am sharing this because, just like my cousin, naturally, we spiritually have an enemy. He plans attacks against us. He is the source of all rivals. He is looking to take us out, but thank God. We have one that walks through life with us. He's never lost a battle. He's undefeated. His name is Jesus! When we operate knowing no matter what, I'm not alone. Our mindset concerning rivals change. We will enter a battle from a place of victory!

Joseph did not give life to the things that went wrong in his world. I believe this with my whole heart. I believe he held close to the promises of God concerning him. How can I be so sure, you may ask? As I've read, I noticed his BELIEF through his service, actions, and overall attitude during every WRONGED season he faced.

How can you shift your mindset as you prepare for the battles of life?

_____

_____

_____

_____

_____

_____

_____

_____

_____

_____

_____

_____

_____

_____

_____

_____

_____

_____

_____

_____

_____

_____

_____

Day of the One

When you know in your KNOWER what God has spoken is true, NOTHING can bring defeat in your life. Nothing can get you to curse your God. Nothing can stop you from speaking and believing his word. Nothing will keep you from operating in the gift. Nothing will keep you from serving and loving people. Not even a prison. Joseph's perspective he later shared with his brothers, sums up my very thoughts.

"You intended to harm me, but God intended it for good to accomplish what is now being done, the saving of many lives." Genesis 50:20 NIV. Now, that's a KNOWING!

I'm just coming into this thought myself, so don't think I've mastered this area. Remember, we're doing this study together. I may face storms, seasons, or battles, but the truth is, I am never alone, and all things work together for my good. These names (storms, seasons, and battles) will not find their heartbeats by my spoken words or breath. I am choosing to believe and, again, only believe. Lord, let this truth be shown in my actions as with your servant Joseph. Amen.

What do you KNOW that God has spoken to you about
your life?

_____

_____

_____

_____

_____

_____

_____

_____

_____

_____

_____

_____

_____

_____

_____

_____

_____

Day of Waiting Again, Lord

There was a season that I decided not to wait. Although I tasted the goodness of the Lord, it was not enough. I even experienced his promises being fulfilled in my life, but it was not enough. I decided his TIMING was not good enough. Due to my impatience and trying to make my own way, I grew weary and almost fainted. It's only by His grace that I stand today. Waiting is protection, not a punishment or a prison. Choose to wait.

Be encouraged! Wait on the Lord. He will RENEW your strength. He will cause you to mount on wings like the eagle and soar. You will run and not grow weary; you shall walk and not faint. Isaiah 40:31

In what areas do you hear God telling you to wait on Him?

_____

_____

_____

_____

_____

_____

_____

_____

_____

_____

_____

_____

_____

_____

_____

_____

_____

_____

_____

Day of Friendship

I was sitting and thinking this morning about how grateful I am. I walked through a dark season. There are blessings from that season, for sure. One is, knowing that God is still bringing his people out of darkness and leading us into his marvelous light. If you are in darkness, keep pushing, for your light has come Isaiah 60:1! Be encouraged.

Next, the necessity of having quality FRIENDS in my life. I thank God for those in my life who not only understand me emotionally but can understand me spiritually. I value those that speak from the spirit when I'm EMOTIONAL! It hurts, yet I greatly appreciate it. Our feelings together can promote reasons for me to stay longer in a pity party.

Please don't misunderstand; I'm not saying a friend should be out of tune with my afflictions or victories. Proverbs 17:17 says a friend loves at all times. When I cry, yes, CRY. When I shout, yes, SHOUT. But, when the rubber meets the road, please remember, it's the TRUTH that sets me free. As a friend, tell the truth in love. The only truth that remains on earth is what the BIBLE says. That's what I need when life goes south. I am thankful for my tribe. We do this thing called "LIFE" together. No LIFE left behind!

Who are the friends in your life who support you in this way?

_____

_____

_____

_____

_____

_____

_____

_____

_____

_____

_____

_____

_____

_____

_____

_____

_____

_____

_____

Day of Face to Face

Sunflowers are heliotropic, which means that they turn their flowers to follow the movement of the sun across the sky from east to west and then return at night to face the east, ready again for the morning sun.

What are you facing this morning? When we don't turn our heads to face the SON, we forget what He has said about us. It's the TURNING that makes the difference. As women, we take on so many roles (wife, mother, sister, cousin, nurse/doctor, team mom, unpaid Uber driver, chef, teacher, housekeeper, etc.) that pulls for our attention. Instead of facing the SON, we can find ourselves facing ROLES. These roles sometimes become the very things we begin to identify ourselves with. Are they really you? Do they define you?

God forbid if all those titles were taken away, what would remain? Trust me; there is no judgment here. I had engulfed myself in those roles to the point of losing myself. I have no fingers to point at you. I'm just asking the hard questions.

Who are you? Do you know? Will you be like the sunflower with seeds to continue to produce growth?

What has your attention?

Do you need to turn your head towards the SON?

Day of What I Know

1. There is no rivalry when we know who we are.
2. Speak life into yourself
3. I can/I am messages, or simply our WORDS, are the secret to being confident and sufficient in Christ's sufficiency in every circumstance.

Paul said,
I know how to get along and live humbly [in difficult times], and I also know how to enjoy abundance and live in prosperity. In any and every circumstance, I have learned the secret [of facing life], whether well-fed or going hungry, whether having an abundance or being in need.

Philippians 4:12 AMP
I can do all things [which He has called me to do] through Him who strengthens and empowers me [to fulfill His purpose—I am self-sufficient in Christ's sufficiency; I am ready for anything and equal to anything through Him who infuses me with inner strength and confident peace.]

Philippians 4:13 AMP
My "I can, I am" message matches Paul's....
I can DO ALL THINGS through Christ
I am SELF-SUFFICIENT in Christ's sufficiency
I am READY for anything
I am EQUAL to anything (no comparison.... WHAT???)

The secret is out! Now, go be GREAT in Christ!

Write your I CAN statements here.